BRITAIN IN PICTURES

THE BRITISH PEOPLE IN PICTURES

WILD LIFE OF BRITAIN

GENERAL EDITOR

W. J. TURNER

★

The Editor is most grateful to all those who have so kindly helped in the selection of illustrations, especially to officials of the various public Museums, Libraries and Galleries, and to all others who have generously allowed pictures and MSS. to be reproduced.

WILD LIFE OF BRITAIN

F. FRASER DARLING

WITH
8 PLATES IN COLOUR
AND
29 ILLUSTRATIONS IN
BLACK & WHITE

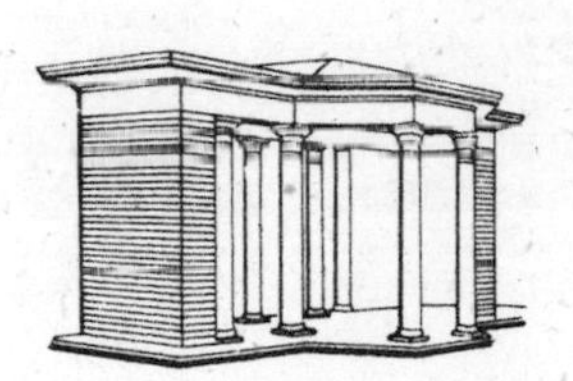

WILLIAM COLLINS OF LONDON
MCMXXXXIII

PRODUCED BY
ADPRINT LIMITED LONDON

★

PRINTED
IN GREAT BRITAIN BY
WM. COLLINS SONS AND CO. LTD. GLASGOW

LIST OF ILLUSTRATIONS

PLATES IN COLOUR

BLACK & WHITE ILLUSTRATIONS

VIGNETTE

Special acknowledgment must be made to the authorities of the Zoological Society of London by whose courtesy all the illustrations not otherwise acknowledged have been made available

SQUIRREL
Lithograph from William Daniell's *Animated Nature*, 1809

THE COUNTRY

An American cowboy on his first visit to Britain sat amazed as he looked from the windows of his railway carriage on this journcy from Plymouth to London.

"But where are all the people?" he asked.

The cowboy was accustomed to the spaces of the range States; he accepted populous cities like New York, Chicago and Seattle as a small part of the vast American scene, but with the love of his countrymen for facts and figures he had doubtless compared the size of Britain with America in the pages of his Atlas and learned that in this small country there was the extraordinarily dense human population of over 640 to the square mile—more than one person for every acre of ground in the kingdom! His mind had conjured a vision of some extended Piccadilly or Bolton with few horizons beyond those of a Trafalgar Square or at best a Hyde Park.

And here he was passing through English country, the railway taking as if by intention a route that showed the beauty and variety of that which is England. The train skirted the high and rugged plateau of Dartmoor, an empty-seeming place from the carriage windows, through a cathedral city called Exeter which was surely not as big as Laramie, Wyoming; on again through the lush meadows and little woodlands of Somerset where he saw a woman milking a Channel Island cow as it stood quiet in the pasture, and before long he was high into Wiltshire where the wide downlands stretch away to Salisbury Plain. London was less than a hundred miles away and still the scene was rural. The closely-banked houses and the masses of people must start soon—but no, even within twenty miles of London there were woods and fields and gay gardens.

I do not know what the cowboy thought of London and it is hardly likely he spent his time seeking that part of the Capital which yet holds a host of wild living things. Perhaps he saw a cormorant perched on the cross above St. Paul's, or a moorhen may have stepped about his feet as he sat in St. James's Park, but it is doubtful if he saw the black redstart in Westminster or the blue butterflies flitting across London's commons.

It is one of the paradoxes of this little Atlantic archipelago of British Islands that with its masses of people and murky industrial areas it still contains stretches of deep rural country, commons, fens and wastes untouched for a thousand years, and mountains and moors which are wild, remote and little trodden by man. We have thousands of miles of sea coast, some of it as wild as any in the world and which also holds a wild life as magnificent of its kind as anything in the world. We are a paradoxical people indeed, for we are mostly kind to animals, though we hunt some of them with a fervour and ritual almost religious. Our standard of care for domesticated animals is as high as any and higher than many in Europe, and our distinctive literature of natural history shows us as an observant and sympathetic folk, yet as a nation we coldly see the ribbon development of our countryside and laconically accept the extinction of one more member of our small but interesting island fauna.

And here is another paradox: the cowboy saw empty acres and asked where were the people; he had unconsciously put his finger on the sociological fact that despite its rural tradition, Britain is an urban country—the great majority of its people live in towns and there is a continual tendency towards urbanization, so that many rural areas actually contain fewer people than years ago. All this movement of men, the changes in activities resulting from it and the constant increase in numbers have a profound effect on the wild life which shares the countryside with us, whether bird, beast or flower. The rural dweller is in general little bothered about the wild life round him and his knowledge of living things outside his immediate orbit is surprisingly small and inaccurate. Taken as a whole, it is the town dweller who has tried to awaken the national conscience and consciousness to the beauty of our countryside with its heritage of wild life. It is as if the rural tradition had fermented a burning nostalgia in the heart of urban men and women, which state has in turn evoked a positive will to do and conserve that which remains. Sometimes this love of living things has suffused the mind of a whole district where the wild life is particularly rich and beautiful, and then we have a glimpse of a countryside that could be, not some vast game reserve from which the human animal alone is debarred, but what the biologist calls a habitat—a place where men and other living things share the same ground and attain to a way of living together in tolerance and amity.

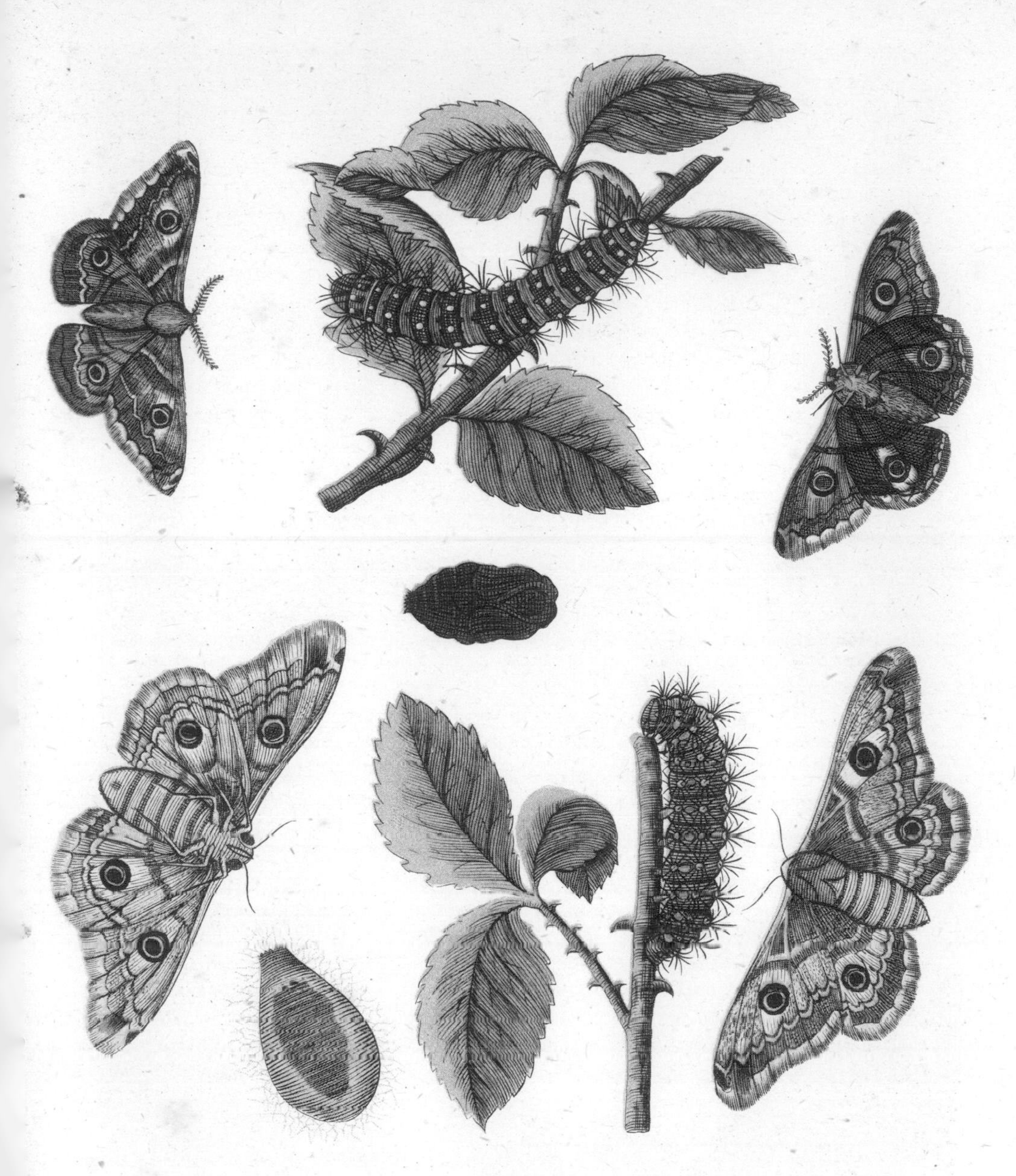

EMPEROR MOTH
Coloured engraving by Terasson after Albin
From Eleazer Albin's *Natural History of English Insects,* 1749

By courtesy of Fores & Co., London

PHEASANT SHOOTING NEAR UXBRIDGE

Coloured aquatint by R. Havell

The wonder and character of Britain is in the country's variety, placed in a northern latitude and given an oceanic climate by the Atlantic Drift. A physical map shows some of this variety of conformation, but it is illuminating at the same time to look at the coloured geological map of Britain, which in itself is a decorative thing because of the prodigal wealth of different rocks which are the bones of our country. Maps showing details of soil and vegetation are at last being made, but even without their help it is possible to say that the rock formations in their wild variety largely dictate the nature of the life which grows upon them, not only of the vegetation but of beast, bird and insect as well. A Martian gazing on the face of Britain might well choose this country for a living museum.

There are the bleak moors of granite and millstone grit in Devon and Cornwall where the red deer still live wild, and there is the almost sub-tropical splendour of the sheltered hollows by the sea at the southern foot of the moors ; the chalk downs stretch from Dorset to Kent and enfold the woods and heaths of the New Forest, a stretch of country marvellously rich in insect life, of which the butterflies alone are evident jewels ; the Thames Valley is rich in birds and beasts and the wide acres of Midland grass with their well kept hedges and ditches and quiet thickets are themselves a field where shy beasts roam at night and in the early morning—badger, fox, weasel and otter ; fieldmouse, squirrel and vole—all are there in fair plenty. East Anglia and Lincolnshire contain much highly farmed ground and the fields are so large that there is not that profusion of hedges and thickets which make the Midlands and the South a safe home for a large number of the passerine birds ; and mechanized arable cultivation tends to deplete the numbers of ground-nesting birds like peewits, corncrakes and larks. Yet in these eastern counties there are fens, broads and marshes which are a birdwatcher's paradise and contain species not found elsewhere in Britain. The bittern is there and breeding, ruff and reeve are regularly seen and the lucky watcher may see the avocet, that most beautiful wader which we have lost as a breeding species. East Anglia is probably the finest place for wildfowl in Britain. The shallow waters and mudbanks of the Wash are a sanctuary for thousands of common seals—not a sanctuary by man's consent because these animals are a nuisance when present in too large numbers, but the Wash is a perfect vantage ground for them and these wily animals are safe from the gunner. The meres and mudflats of Cheshire on the other side of England are also a great reservoir and resting place for a rich and varied bird and insect life. The topographical position of this area, flanked as it is by the industrial districts of the Mersey and Lancashire, has caused it to be somewhat overlooked as a home and sanctuary of wild life.

Wales has not such a rich avian fauna as England, though on its west coast and among the few small islands there are fine cliffs of sea birds. Many migrants pass through that part of Wales and one of the most interesting sides of R. M. Lockley's work on the island of Skokholm has been his recording of migrants through the trap he has built there. The little islet of Grassholm with its 6,000 gannets is the most southerly breeding station in Britain of a species in which more than half the total world population is British. Off south-west Wales and

COMMON SEAL
Water colour drawing by A. Thorburn reproduced in his *British Mammals*, 1920

off the Cornish coast across the Bristol Channel, the Atlantic grey seal is still fairly plentiful, though the so-called common seal is not found. The Black Mountains of Wales are now the only place in Britain where kites live, and despite rigorous protection it is likely the species will die out, for the numbers are insufficient to maintain the birds in dynamic breeding state. Snowdonia and the mountains round about form a reservoir of beautiful plants not found elsewhere in England and Wales. When collectors kill birds and take their eggs, they and everyone else should know it is a crime against society, but the person with a rock garden feels few qualms of conscience in taking plants from the mountains, because he takes the view he is not killing but perpetuating. But so few of these little saxifrages and primulas do survive in the rockeries of those who take them (and I have rarely heard of a successful gardener returning surplus plants to new places in the mountains) that there is need for care of these Welsh outposts of our island flora. The country of the Welsh Marches is not densely populated and there is a lot of thin woodland and scrubby ground providing a home for many of our wild mammals. It is only in Wales, also, that the polecat may be found, for it is now generally considered extinct in the Lake District and in Scotland.

The industrial North of England gives a bleak prospect for wild life. Numbers of people alone are an inhibiting factor, and smoke and fumes of chemicals are hurtsome to plant life which must be the basis of a fauna. Nevertheless, it is a characteristic of life to press its distribution to its utmost limits, and with the help of the mountainous nature of the Pennine Chain running between Lancashire and Yorkshire, a variety of wild living things thrive alongside and near the masses of humanity and their belching chimneys. Look for example at the steep sides

of ... landscape of
li ... nd from every
ni ... ure and happy,
sp ... rds. And on
th ... will never see
a ... nperor moths.

2.15 I YSGOLION CYMRU. (For Welsh schools). 'Hanes Cymru'. Cyfres i

turns to its usual place in the 'Farming Today' programme

Time, Greenwich: NEWS

'ACE-FLIERS AMONG THE BIRDS', about which Scott Kennedy will give a nature study talk for Schools this afternoon at 2.0. From left to right are: male sparrow-hawk, male kestrel, and female peregrine falcon.

GANNET
Aquatint from Daniell's *Animated Nature*, 1809

The moths of the Pennine slopes are of particular interest in the large number of melanic variations they provide.

The Lake District is a natural sanctuary for the North of England. There are a few red deer there and until recently the pine marten still lived a changed life among the rocks of the wilder hills. The char, a fish of the salmon tribe, which is a relic of glacial times, is still to be found in the deep, cold waters of Windermere and some other lakes in the area. Buzzards soar over Lakeland slopes, but not the golden eagle—she seems to have gone for good from England.

Sheep farming and forestry are the principal industries of the hills of the Scottish Border and neither is conducive to the maintenance of a rich wild life. Roe deer and black grouse are killed off in the early years of a coniferous plantation and later the stands are too dense to serve as a desirable habitat. The short grazing and regular burning of the sheep ground keeps it bare. Field voles and blue hares are plentiful in this kind of country and occasionally increase to the level of being a plague ; then the normal population of predatory animals like kestrels, buzzards, ravens, owls, stoats and weasels increases also. Such helpful creatures normally live a less hunted life on the greentop hills, for on the black-top or heathery hills the red grouse lives and is protected by all means as an object of sport.

The Scottish Lowlands are surprisingly full of birds and beasts, though the northern latitude is beginning to have its effect on variety as compared with the South of England. The nightingale is not heard, nor many of the warblers which delight the listener in a Surrey woodland. But the Tweed Valley and Estuary

GOLDEN EAGLE
Aquatint from Daniell's *Animated Nature*, 1809

and the Firth of Forth are great places for ducks and wading birds of many kinds. The Bass Rock in the Firth is a big gannetry, and just south of the eastern Border are the Farne Islands, now a sanctuary for sea birds and for the only colony of Atlantic seals to be found on the east side of Britain.

North again to the Highlands and Islands there is a further reduction in variety of small birds, of moths and butterflies and of some of the mammals. This fact is compensated, however, by the new northern species not found south of the Highland Line. The red stag may be seen on most mountains and roe deer are plentiful. Wild cats have always persisted in the deer-forest country and have extended their range in recent years. It is a fine sight to see a pair of golden eagles soaring above some high corrie, seeking the mountain blue hares which form the bulk of their food when these small beasts are plentiful. Highland stalkers have no wish to exterminate the eagle, but they do limit numbers, and the eagle is not a difficult bird to kill. When an eagle is found to be taking young lambs, its days are numbered. The foxes of the Highlands are ruthlessly hunted with terrier dog and gun for the toll on lambs and deer calves is very high. Nevertheless, this animal persists and his rise and fall in numbers is much more influenced by disease than by the activities of man.

It is on Highland lochs that the black- and red-throated diver is found and some of the less common grebes. And at rare points among the islands there are still small colonies of the red-necked phalarope, that dainty little wading bird which changes over between male and female the normal parental duties. The female has the brighter plumage and courts the male, and once she has laid the eggs it is he who incubates them. These same wild peat bogs of the Outer Isles, bestrewn with lochs and difficult of passage by man, hold the last considerable number of breeding grey-lag geese, the only species of goose breeding in Britain. There are a few more grey-lags breeding on the far northern mainland of Scotland, but they do not extend to the Orkney and Shetland Isles. The northern island groups hold some magnificent cliffs of sea birds, and such remote islands as St. Kilda and North Rona are breath-taking in their early summer wonder and beauty. Hundreds of thousands of guillemots, razorbills, puffins, fulmar petrels and kittiwakes throng the cliffs and cry out their ecstasy till the observer himself is caught up in the excitement. Three rocks of the St. Kilda group hold 16,900 pairs of gannets : to see that towering white cone of Stac Lii in June is to have gazed on one of the wonders of the world ; or again to have lain awake through a summer night on North Rona or Sula Sgeir when the Leach's fork-tailed petrels have come in from the sea to indulge in their aerial dance and wild crying—this is to have lived. The high, heathery headlands of Shetland above the seething bird cliffs are the home of the great skua, a large brown gull-like bird which pirates its food from all and sundry. Its perfect control of flight is a fine thing to watch. What the north loses in variety it makes up by its few distinctive species and the wild beauty of them in the breeding season.

The Atlantic grey seal is most common on the western and northern fringe of Scotland, more common than anywhere else in the world, for it is one of the rarest of seals. It has been my good fortune to have lived with them on North Rona, which is the breeding ground of perhaps half the world population of these seals. Some of the little islands off the North-West Highland coast have become natural sanctuaries for the otter which has here taken wholly to sea fishing. The animals are rather bigger and thicker coated than the mainland type.

MARTEN
Etching from St. John's *Natural History and Sport in Moray*, 1882

WILD CAT STALKING MOUNTAIN HARES
Lithograph by Wolf from Millais' *Mammals of Great Britain and Ireland*, 1904-1906

THE CREATURES

LET us glance over some of the animals which share the land and sea with us: how do they live their lives and what are the facts of their little civilizations? It surprises many people to learn that we have seventy five species and sub-species of native mammals, a number almost as great as a thousand years ago, for within historical time we have lost only the wolf, the beaver, the wild boar, the brown bear and the reindeer, one fifteenth of the total. Numbers of many species are now much restricted, so is their distribution, and it is possible that some kinds are more wary than in the past, though where sanctuary is given animals soon become easier of approach. Surprise at the number of species comes from the fact that we see so little of most of our mammals as compared with our much richer bird life. Quite half our mammals live a more or less underground existence during the hours of daylight and are busy only when most folk are abed.

The mole lives wholly underground and to arrive at a true picture of its habits the observer has to upset the everyday life of several colonies. Here is an animal showing extremes of adaptation to a subterranean existence—scarcely functioning eyes, fore feet as efficient as mechanical navvies and a fur showing no bias of direction. It would be difficult for the mole to change in this changing Britain, yet it persists and has extended its range remarkably. How indeed does the mole

WATER SHREW
Engraving from Thomas Pennant's *British Zoology*, 1812

cross the high mountain passes over the backbone of Scotland? It is not the individual who gets there, but the species, in the course of time, like the frogs I have found sometimes on mountain tops.

All our mice prefer nocturnal activity and spend the days out of sight and so do those animals which prey on them. How often have I, moving through a Highland forest at night to keep check of the movements of deer at that time, bewailed my inability to see as the animals do, for I have caught fugitive glances of the tremendous animal activity of the night without being able to piece it all together.

Over twenty mammals live in the sea and are not visible except when they come up to breathe—the whales, dolphins and porpoises—though one who lives by the sea may gain stimulating sidelights on the habits of these creatures. From remote island shores I have seen a whale scratch his back against a cliff below water, a school of dolphins leaping from the sea in wild play and a porpoise that barked was in our anchorage for several days.

There are twelve species of bats, all night-flying, thus denying us opportunity of observing in detail their food-getting habits. In daytime and in winter the bats roost in belfries and caves and places where the average person does not go, so we know little of this sixth part of our mammalian fauna.

Birdwatching requires patience if it is to be well done, but to watch the intimate daily life of mammals calls for much more. The red deer may take you to remote parts and move quickly over rough country, the badger may keep you waiting all night near his sett and never emerge, the wild cat will lie silent and unseen along the branch of a pine tree or in the long heather and leave you little trace of his being in the country at all, and in order to watch a water shrew's family life you will first have to find the animals and then only from brief spells spent in the open may its behaviour be certainly inferred. Many mammals are less active in winter than in summer and some as far apart in the zoological scale

HARVEST MICE
Lithograph by P. J. Smit
From *The Royal Natural History*, edited by R. Lydekker, 1895

STAG BEETLE
Lithograph from Daniell's *Animated Nature*, 1809

as badger, hedgehog and dormouse, become torpid in November and hibernate for several months. If you are going to watch animals, it is best to go for one at a time and by yourself and if other incidents are seen they can be accepted as the jam on the plain bread-and-butter of observation. Thus, of a summer night, seeking the ways of the long-tailed field mouse through an English oak wood, you will hear rabbits stamping their warning through the telegraph of the earth, a fox may pad by almost noiselessly in the long grass and bracken which is growing through last year's carpet of leaves; Brock the badger may come scraping among the leaves, a rabbit's squeal will tell of the stoat busy at the constant work of filling his belly—like those we have seen already—and like the noiseless bats flitting after insects between the trees above our heads. When we see the animals of the night abroad they are usually seeking food, but sometimes they come before us in the spontaneity of play. Our hearts warm to them for they are happy, with the possible drudgery of food-getting momentarily forgotten, and in play we can approach them nearer in understanding, for the human animal is himself one of the most playful—at least, if he is being himself and not trying to be someone he thinks he ought to be! To see British mammals means both good luck and hard work, but the work is worth while.

There are many more amateur watchers of birds than of mammals, not only for the reasons just given, but because there are over four hundred species of birds on the British List. Birds are mobile creatures, many being migratory, and lots more visit this country only occasionally. Thus birdwatching partakes of the

DRAGONFLY
Lithograph from Daniell's *Animated Nature*, 1809

nature of a sport in that undoubted surprises are to be had in the course of a season's work. Butterflies, moths and dragonflies are the most spectacular of the thousands of kinds of insects which populate the earth with us, and because of their visual prominence and beauty they do receive some kindly regard from the citizen. There are only seventy-five British butterflies, several hundreds of moths and a mere handful of dragonflies. There are about five thousand beetles in Britain, some useful to husbandry, some harmful, but most of them neutral and living their lives unseen. Yet the iridescence of a beetle's wing case is one of the loveliest things to be found under a stone. Two-winged flies are more numerous and obvious than the beetles and there are nearly as many species. These are the basic food supply of much of our other wild life.

Britain has few reptiles. There is one poisonous snake, the adder, and two harmless ones, the grass snake and the ringed snake. And we have only two lizards, a cheerful little brown fellow who adds to the charm of many a waste place and a wall lizard found in Dorset and Lancashire. The slowworm is a legless lizard sometimes mistaken for a snake and thoughtlessly killed, but its activities are wholly useful. Our amphibians are also few—the frog, two toads and three newts.

All these things are much affected by the results of human activities such as agriculture, fen drainage, and industrial expansion with its consequent pollution of air and water. And how little a thing will help the creatures we love best—last year I fenced a length of cliff as an insurance against the cattle going over and to allow a few trees to grow there: this simple act let all grasses and wild flowers grow in their own way unhindered except as food plants for caterpillars, and this year that cliff top is brilliant with the flight of common blue, green-veined white, dark green fritillary and meadow brown butterflies.

Over two thousand species make up the British flora and these again are much at the mercy of man, who does not so much directly destroy as render a habitat untenable for some plants by his varied activities. Many of our rarest and most beautiful plants have little or no place as animal food, but we must remember that vegetation is at the base of the whole pyramid of wild life. And not only as food: plants show immense variety in type and habitat and provide a large measure of the topography of a countryside. Cover means much in animal life—for the predator catching its quarry, for the quarry hiding from the predator and as a factor ameliorating climate. So man in his control of vegetation wields a fateful sword in the lives of the rest of the animal world.

BOTTLE-NOSED DOLPHIN
Pen drawing by Thorburn from his *British Mammals*, 1920

STUDIES OF BADGERS

Pen drawings by J. G. Millais from his *Mammals of Great Britain and Ireland*, 1904-1906

WEASELS
Engraving from Bingley's *Memoirs of British Quadrupeds*, 1809

HISTORY AND NATURAL HISTORY

A MODERN appraisal of a country's wild life is no dull catalogue of numbers of species. It should be a summary of the innumerable facts comprising the one great fact of man and many other living things inhabiting the same ground, making, maintaining and breaking equilibria, battling and co-operating, acting consciously and unconsciously. Such an appraisal must be to some extent a history of ideas—of the changes from man the hunter for the pot, through the periods of man the hunter for fun, to the time of man the hunter for knowledge, the controller for his own continued existence and the conserver for love.

Man the hunter was an intensely aware human being. He was at one with the wild life about him as few men are to-day. His awareness was practical, not intellectual. He saw things and understood them in their relation to one another and we may reasonably believe he saw his world as a beautiful place in his own way. Though he hunted to kill he did not appear to lose respect for his quarry, for the anthropologist has disclosed how high a place animal life took in the primitive social structure of totem and tabu. A hunting community of that kind does not destroy the wild life of its area ; it merely takes toll like the rest of the predatory animals. But as soon as agriculture begins, a new defensive and offensive

WILD OR WHITE FOREST BREED: BULL FROM CHILLINGHAM PARK
Coloured lithograph after a painting by Shiels
From David Low's *Domestic Animals of the British Isles*, 1842

attitude is adopted towards wild life. An animal which is the quarry of the hunter arouses no feeling of antipathy, but the deer which raid the crops of the husbandman become a definite enemy. The written word appeared long after man was a farmer and through literature we find man suspicious of animals in general as possible takers of what he has got or of what he is growing. Having lost so much of the hunter's intimate knowledge he preferred to be on the safe side and not give the animal the benefit of the doubt. No one ever saw a hedgehog sucking milk from a cow but it was very firmly believed that it did, and the poor little beast whose general activities were so helpful to man was consistently killed until almost our own time.

Concomitant with what may be called the agricultural view of wild animals there grew a new ritual of hunting, a formalized artificial activity which invested certain animals with the title and sanctity of 'game.' Red deer, wild boar, hares, pheasants, grouse, partridges, black grouse, corncrakes, salmon and trout were all termed game and their hunting was reserved for royalty and such landholders as were granted the king's favour. Even the seas were not free for fishing salmon and to-day it still remains along with the sturgeon the king's fish. Those who own salmon rights on coast and river hold the grant direct from the crown. The right to hunt game was gradually extended until an owner of ten contiguous acres could take game. Now it is merely a matter of paying three guineas for a game licence and getting an invitation to shoot over someone else's acres if you have none of your own.

Another group of animals came to be more or less arbitrarily classed as vermin and could be killed by anyone—sometimes to the accompaniment of receiving a bounty—wolf, polecat, badger, fox, marten, stoat, weasel, otter, wild cat, crow, raptorial birds and so on. But some of these animals, particularly the fox and the otter, gradually came to be hunted in formal fashion by the upper classes and thus gathered some of the exclusive tone of game animals. Hunting was no longer a matter of filling the pot with the joy of hunting incidental; it was fun first and the pot either a poor second or left out altogether. Recent years have seen the list of vermin somewhat altered. No sensible man shoots kestrels to-day; buzzards are rightly coming into their own as one of the best rabbit killers we have; and the rabbit itself, instead of being carefully preserved in warrens, has come definitely to be regarded as vermin. Falconry and hawking were common four hundred years ago and only when these sports died out were the hawks added to the list of vermin.

King Canute was the first English king to set aside large areas of forest land for his own sporting purposes and make a formal charter. William the Conqueror came a few years later and greatly increased the number and extent of the royal forests, protecting them by special and very harsh forest laws. His barons were also able to establish chases for their private sport, but these were protected only by common law.

The barons went to some trouble to herd into their chases anything that was worth having in the way of hoofed beasts such as red and fallow deer and the white feral cattle common in the great forests of Saxon times. The effect of all this was profound for our own day, though the men of England did not take kindly to such absolutism. It is not the English way and before many years had passed we see the forests and the chases being whittled down and the rights of the people steadily growing as part of the evolution of England. These game preserves for the exercise and pleasure of the privileged class soon became small islands in the agricultural and unenclosed land and common grazings. Some of them persist to-day, much attenuated but still containing the descendants of some of those animals originally herded into and protected in the forests and chases. Windsor Great Park, the New Forest, Savernake Forest, Epping Forest; Cannock Chase, Chillingham Park, Chatsworth Park, Cadzow Park and several more. In these places are found red deer of stronger type than the truly wild specimens of Dartmoor and Exmoor, the English Lakes and the Scottish Highlands, and in Chillingham and Cadzow there remain almost the last small herds of wild white cattle, beautiful shy creatures which can hardly be expected to persist much longer. Those of Chillingham have lately come to be supported in part by the British public through the Zoological Society of London.

The wild boar disappeared from Britain in the 16th century, despite the elaborate sport he provided. His depredations on a growing agriculture must have been so great that common sense prevailed over privilege. The wolf may or may not have provided sport, but every man's hand was against this beast and he

STICKLEBACKS

Coloured lithograph by A. F. Lydon.

From Houghton's *British Fresh-water Fishes*, 1879

By courtesy of Frederick Warne & Co., Ltd.

A SALMON LEAP

Coloured lithograph by P. J. Smit

From *The Royal Natural History,* edited by R. Lydekker, 1895

was extinct in England in the 17th century and in Scotland in the 18th. These early preserves were absolutely protected for the pleasure of the hunter but not managed in the more modern sense of gamekeeping for the increase of the animals. The formalism and punctilio of sport did in itself exercise some management in the way of close seasons and certain beasts being "warrantable" and others not, but that was all. Herons might not be taken except with hawks, for example, nor were pheasants to be taken at night. It has become a definite part of the English sporting tradition to kill only in certain ways and at certain times, and whatever our views on the ethics of blood sports, we cannot fail to be thankful for the permeation of this old tradition through the whole fabric of English life. It is part of our notion of fair play, warped at times sure enough, but nevertheless there.

Henry VIII instituted definite measures for the conservation of wild life in his ban on taking waterfowl or their eggs during June, July and August. He also established a bounty (to be paid by the landowners) on birds of the crow tribe which were hard on eggs and young birds. James I extended this kind of law and there gradually evolved the artificial, but nevertheless purely empirical, methods of raising stocks of game on private estates. Game became almost deified and vermin were execrated, but between these two groups of creatures lay the bulk of our beautiful wild life, sometimes gaining from the protection of game and sometimes losing in the suppression of predatory animals. Taken all in all, we may believe British wild life benefitted during the period of industrial expansion by the jealous guarding of the hunting playgrounds of the privileged classes. The rich and powerful were not preserving wild life *ad hoc*, but they were preserving habitats, and that was of immense value.

We should remember also that industrialism had something to offer to wild life in the creation of stretches of water, water in reservoirs as the supplies of large cities, water in canals and in the reservoirs of canal companies. Take for example the Grand Junction Canal Reservoir north of Tring, Hertfordshire; this is a relatively dry part of Britain and exceptionally lacking in areas of water, yet it is a place where many a bird-watcher sees his ducks and waders. Sewage farms are not counted romantic places but more than a few suburban Londoners spend their Sunday mornings watching the filters at Staines, where rare birds are attracted during the migratory periods. Surrey is one of the best haunts of wild life in Britain, and to this reputation the ponds of the old-time Surrey ironworkers have contributed. I know also of a dull and drear expanse of water set between colliery slag heaps in the Central Plain of Scotland. Land is good there and if this place could be drained and farmed it would be, but it cannot be done economically, and just before the war the Scottish Nature Reserves Committee was taking special measures to ensure the safety of the abundant wild life attracted to this place and which gave pleasure to the vast majority of the working folk in the neighbourhood.

There can be no doubt that minds and consciences were beginning to work during the growing period of industrialism: it is the period when the study of natural history began for the love of it and in 1831 an Act of Parliament was passed protecting certain birds which were not game. A bird sanctuary was first decreed by Parliament in 1869 and since then there has been a slowly growing tendency for public bodies to prevent hunting or killing in certain places and to suppress such methods of vermin control as are indiscriminate. Pole traps, for example, were prohibited in 1904 and the use of bird lime in 1925. Most of the facts I have given in this paragraph would be difficult to find tabulated in any English publication and I am indebted to the American book by Aldo Leopold, *Game Management* as a source of this summary.

All these methods of protection were in effect passive, though the gradual change of outlook from king and baron preserving game for their own fun to an awakening public beginning to take care of wild life for its own sake was very sure progress. Let us look for a few moments at the type of man who helped to bring about the change, the naturalist as he was called, a type of explorer in the early days and a sincere seeker after truth. Such a type has persisted to this day and has acquired a new vigour through application of the science of ecology—the study of organisms in relation to their environment—but it must be added that the twentieth century has produced another type of naturalist as well, the writer of sentimental, anthropomorphic nonsense who degrades the status of wild-life conservation.

HEDGEHOG
Pen drawing from Thorburn's *British Mammals*, 1920

THE PLEYSTOW, SELBORNE
Engraving from Gilbert White's *History and Antiquities of Selborne*, 1789

THE NATURALISTS

THERE were a few very early naturalists, but Gilbert White of Selborne, 1720-1793, was the first of the modern school of close and accurate observers. Here was a man of good family and education who preferred to stay in his birthplace as curate of the parish rather than accept more ambitious livings. Gilbert had the seeing eye and he loved his place ; he knew it year in, year out, all his life, and was always finding something new and worthy of record. That is the way to know country—live in it, love it, record minutely and use your notes to keep your memory green and pliant. Had this great naturalist been mock modest he would not have recorded, but his was the true humility which knew its own worth. He had a definite idea of what he thought a "parochial history" should be and had the conviction to record to that end. But there was no effort whatever to present the naturalist himself, for most of his valuable and original observations were written in letters to Thomas Pennant and the Hon. Daines Barrington. Pennant was a good naturalist, not as good as White, though he had the right feeling of the time to get information set down in ordered form. To this end Pennant wrote *British Zoology*, 1768-1770, and *History of Quadrupeds*, 1781, which became the classic works of the period, and in these books he acknowledges the curate of Selborne as the source of much information. The inspiration of Gilbert White for British countrymen is evergreen ; one of the earliest societies for the preservation of wild life in this country was the Selborne Society founded in 1887. The tradition of British natural history set by White may be summed up in this short quotation from a letter to Barrington in 1771 :

> Faunists, as you observe, are too apt to acquiesce in their descriptions, and a few synonyms : the reason is plain ; because all that may be done at home in a man's study, but the investigation of the life and conversation of animals is a concern of much more trouble and difficulty, and is not to be attained but by the active and inquisitive, and by those that reside much in the country.

My friend James Fisher has pointed in a companion volume to the influence on natural history of the English and Scottish clergy of the eighteenth and nineteenth centuries. They were scholarly men given to recording, and in the nineteenth century many of them blossomed as naturalists. There was F. O. Morris who produced a six-volumed work of *British Birds* with coloured plates of every species ; C. E. Johns who published works on birds and flowers, J. G. Wood, author of many popular books, and nearer our own time and more scientific there have been Pickard Cambridge, the authority on spiders, and F. C. R. Jourdain who has died during the period of production of the new *Handbook of British Birds*, of which he was part author.

Other naturalists of the collecting, recording and compiling period were William Yarrell, 1784-1856, who wrote books on *British Birds* and *British Fishes* which were standard works for a long time, and John Gould, 1804-1881, the Bird Man, whose most famous work *The Birds of Great Britain*, 1862-1873, contained magnificent coloured plates and representations of the young of each species.

The English squire of tradition carried the torch of the ancient hunter and paradoxically loved the animals he hunted. And in the English squire there was rooted the very definite opinion that he was a free man, an opinion which was usually backed by the money and power to be such. Charles Waterton, 1782-1865, was one of these. He did what he wanted to do and cared nothing for convention, whether it was climbing the fabric of St. Peter's in Rome to set a glove on the cross at the summit of the dome (Waterton was a devout Catholic) or climbing a tall tree in his own park at the age of over eighty. We are not concerned here with his good book of natural history entitled *Wanderings in South America* so much as with the fact that he was the first man in England to establish a wild-life sanctuary for sheer love and interest in the animals within it. To this end he built a high wall round the large park of his Yorkshire estate, Walton Hall. That act was a very great break with the rigid conventions of his class, but it was robust and typical of the individual British naturalist arising at this period.

We should not forget another naturalist of the squirearchal type, Charles St. John, 1809-1856, who wrote that classic book *Wild Sports and Natural History of the Highlands*. St. John was an Englishman of good family who found the North of Scotland to be his true home. The Highlands of that period were a wild place into which Mammon and his shooting lodges had not yet stepped.

ADDER
Lithograph by E. Cooke from *British Reptiles* by M. C. Cooke, 1865

St. John gloried in the sport and freedom; he shot and fished and took birds' nests, and indeed killed many a rare bird he should have left at large. But we must judge a man in his own period and not in our own, and if we do that we find an acute and sensitive observer who loved his quarry and the country the beasts inhabited. His book is a fine piece of work by any standard and his pursuit of the Muckle Hart of Glenmore will remain one of the great stories of the red deer. He portrayed a countryside which changed immediately after his death; the day of the St. John is gone, but I believe the spirit of this man is strong in the British naturalists of to-day. They have his eagerness and incisiveness and delight in rough situations.

The greatest naturalist Britain has produced so far has been Charles Darwin, and naturalist he was, first and before he was a man of science. His life story bears very close study, for here was no brilliant boy at school, later carrying all before him at the University. Charles was almost uneducable in the schools of the period though he would learn easily himself when he found anything which interested him. He liked collecting stones, which seemed to fascinate him and a little later he played with chemicals. Shooting over dogs became quite a passion and in such excursions he was able to collect insects and note the habits of living things. Seeing and finding out; that was what interested him.

A sorely troubled father sent him to learn medicine in Edinburgh, but Charles found it all rather dull and was to be found mixing with the fishermen of the Firth of Forth and playing in the rock pools there. Two years later his father suggested the Church as a career and as this would provide fair leisure for natural history,

Charles made sure of his orthodoxy and entered Cambridge University with the utmost difficulty. Even with the low scholastic standards of the period Darwin only just scraped a B.A. degree after three years, for he cut his lectures, hunted beetles as well as foxes and attended Henslow's botanical excursions. This friendship with Henslow resulted in his ultimate appointment as naturalist on H.M.S. *Beagle* which was about to make a world cruise, and shows that he must have impressed this great botanist with his powers of observation and ability to record.

The five-year voyage was the turning point of Darwin's life. He emerged as a self-reliant individual and thinking man. Perhaps it was a good thing that he had to think himself about all he saw in those five years (for there was no one of his own calibre aboard with whom he could discuss) because his ultimate conclusions were his own, uncoloured by reflection from other minds. The man entering upon a research to-day is expected to read up his subject well beforehand, but in natural history this is not always the wisest course. There is often a good case for going into a problem fresh, uninfluenced by the earlier opinions of others. When Darwin came home again it was as a seasoned naturalist in several sciences, particularly geology. He had an enormous mass of facts from his own observations and he had a mind which could take in facts from anywhere and digest them. Thus he gave up the orthodox notion of species separately created, and crystallized the hitherto nebulous theory of evolution by stating the hypothesis of natural selection, the survival of the fittest and modification in descent.

All this appeared in *The Origin of Species* in 1859, a book which shook the intellectual foundations of the world and changed the face of biological science. The book would not have appeared when it did, had not another great naturalist, Alfred Russel Wallace, 1823-1913, reached similar conclusions from his work in Malaya. The two men showed their generosity of soul by giving a joint paper before the Linnean Society in 1858, after which it was incumbent on Darwin to publish in full. This book is not concerned with the controversies which followed and the ultimate acceptance of the Darwinian theory, but with the influence of Darwin's work on the study of natural history in Britain. Naturalists, amateur and professional, went into a fever of collecting and collating and numbers more immured themselves in the laboratory studying physiological and anatomical problems in their bearing on evolution. The study of wild life became something more than fun.

Darwin himself was a naturalist and he never forsook the field and the out-of-doors, but that cannot be said for some of his followers. They became academic zoologists and botanists and rather looked down on mere naturalists as not being scientific men. Nevertheless, a host of minor naturalists arose in the ranks of the people as a result of Darwin's work and though he himself does not appear to have expressed any decided views on the ethics and practice of wild-life conservation, there can be no doubt that his work did have the indirect effect of making people more conscious of the value of our living things. Charles Darwin lives to-day in our hearts and I know that in the course of my own work

CHARLES DARWIN 1809-1882
Etching by Rajon after W. W. Ouless

I have often said to myself, "I wish Darwin could have seen this." Even though he has gone from us he remains contemporary.

British naturalists have frequently been amateurs. Take for example Sir John Lubbock, later Lord Avebury, 1834-1913: though a banker and Member of Parliament he found time to experiment minutely on the behaviour of social insects and published his results in the classic work *Ants, Bees and Wasps*, 1882. He published *On the Senses, Instincts and Intelligence of Animals* in 1888, two botanical works in the '90's and several personal books in the last few years of his life. Lubbock lived in Downe, the village in Kent where Darwin lived, and the two men were good friends and collaborators in biological work. Lubbock's approach to natural history was as valuable as the work he accomplished, for he emphasized what is the job of the naturalist studying wild life—to study animals as individuals and living things and not as mere specimens. His technique in marking insects and getting to know them and their little lives intimately has never been surpassed.

Other amateurs who have become authorities or outstanding contributors are Richard South and W. F. Kirby who worked on British butterflies and moths; G. C. Druce, an Oxford chemist whose researches on our flora earned him the degree of D.L. of Oxford University; Sir Thomas Hudson Beare, Professor of Engineering at Edinburgh, who was, until his recent death, a leading authority on beetles; and Ward Fowler, who discovered the marsh warbler as a British breeding species and who wrote *The Natural History of Kingham* on the model of Gilbert White's parochial history.

And here is a group of Scotsmen, all working in natural history for the love of it during that fertile period of the nineteenth century: William and John Macgillivray, father and son, whose observations in the Outer Hebrides were valuable at a time when little detailed work was being done there; Hugh Miller, the quarryman who became the authority on the geology of the Old Red Sandstone; Stephen Saxby, the doctor of Unst, the northernmost island of Shetland, a member of a family distinguished for accurate observation and recording in Thule. Robert Gray was a bank inspector and produced a good book on the *Birds of the West of Scotland*. And it was he who revivified the Royal Physical Society of Edinburgh and made it a force in Scottish natural history. J. A. Harvie Brown was the leader of a group which surveyed the fauna of Scotland from 1880-1904. His large private means allowed him to journey far and wide over the Highlands and Islands and to produce the classic series of books known as *The Vertebrate Fauna of Scotland*. On his death in 1913, the large library of natural history works he had collected was given to the Royal Scottish Museum, Edinburgh. J. Wilson Dougal was a chemist, but the Hebrides were his playground and before his death in 1936 he had made valuable contributions to the geology and archaeology of the islands as well as constantly observing facts in other branches of natural history.

There have been several British naturalists whose contribution has been literary rather than of original research. Their influence has been great on the

ST. KILDA MICE
Coloured lithograph by P. J. Smit
From *The Proceedings of the Zoological Society*, 1899.

By courtesy of the Council of the Ray Society

COMMON FROGS

Coloured lithograph from Boulenger's *The Tailless Batrachians of Europe*, 1908

aesthetic and ethical attitude of people towards wild life. There was the lazy boy Richard Jefferies, for example, 1848-1887, who had a remarkable power of vividly setting down what his eyes saw. His was no great mind, but one unusually receptive of the natural scene. Such people, born as farmers' sons, are inevitably styled lazy because they stand and stare, or preferably lie and look, and by a farmer's standard that is not being practical. Jefferies was another example of the boy who, starting with a gun, ultimately lays it down for the pen. *The Gamekeeper at Home*, 1878, faithfully records this period of the gun when, intensely enjoying the wholeness of nature, he was indifferent to the creatures he shot. *The Amateur Poacher*, 1879, holds this passage, portraying the change which worked within him:

> My finger felt the trigger, and the least increase of pressure would have been fatal; but in the act I hesitated, dropped the barrel and watched the beautiful bird.
>
> That watching so often stayed the shot that at last it grew to be a habit; the mere simple pleasure of seeing birds and animals when they were quite unconscious that they were being observed being too great to be spoiled by the discharge.

The writings of the last years of Jefferies' short life show the length of his spiritual journey from the hunter to the mystically-minded interpreter of nature.

To me, as I grow older, the development of naturalists' minds becomes as interesting as the natural history they interpret. By what way have they come and whither the new path they are treading? I remember the eager joy with which I found and read the books of William Henry Hudson, 1841-1922, for their facts alone, such books as *The Naturalist in La Plata*, 1892, *Adventures among Birds*, 1913, and the accumulated essays in *The Book of a Naturalist*. Then I read *Green Mansions*, 1904, a story which made such a deep impression that I still put it among my dozen favourite books. Who was this man who could write the secret thoughts of one's own soul?

Rightly, we should question Hudson's inclusion here as a British naturalist for he was born and reared in Argentina. His parents were Americans and he did not become a British subject until 1900, long after he had come to England to live. He had known the pampas in the early free days before enclosures had taken place and when there were vast reserves of wild life. He was a great eagle of a man and a horse's hoofs were his wings. In him again was the power of seeing intensely; his seeing was part of his living like the thrust of the blood.

And then this man comes to an England all prettily hedged and cultivated, and he could interpret that too. But strangest of all he married a woman who kept a boarding house, and settled in a home off the Bayswater Road. Now he began to write and as I see it here is the difference between a caged eagle and a caged eagle of a man. He did not mope and die; he produced out of his poignant nostalgia the living spirit of Rima, the vivid anecdotes of his early life, and as a contrast, *The Shepherd's Life*, a tale of the natural social complex of the Wiltshire Downs.

This caging of the body and its effect on artistic production is a hard thing to accept. Darwin himself was kept at Downe by ill health, Jefferies dictated some of his best essays when he was too weak to hold a pen, and here was Hudson apparently caged voluntarily. Then another young man dying of tuberculosis at twenty-eight shows us a similar intensity of power to see and interpret nature; I am thinking of W. N. P. Barbellion who died in 1919. He was a junior reporter of a local West Country paper but had ever the urge to pursue natural history as a profession. Perhaps his ultimate appointment to the insect room at the British Museum is not everyone's ideal of becoming a naturalist, but a reading of *The Journal of a Disappointed Man* will reveal the depth of his appreciation of nature and the book serves as an indicator of the trend of British thought in relation to wild life at the beginning of the twentieth century.

Let us consider another type of naturalist, the scientific man who is a member of an expedition of discovery. Edward Wilson, 1872-1912, stands out from his fellows because of his great personal goodness and from the circumstances of his death with Captain Scott in the Antarctic. He is the type which has inspired the later generation of naturalists practising to-day—men of scientific training who can approach the problems of animal life analytically and yet not be indifferent to the beauty of the subjects they study, nor devoid of the emotions such beauties arouse.

Edward Wilson was indeed an artist, not only in thought and life, but in painting—some of his drawings and water colours of birds, flowers and animals have never been excelled as such. His pencil and brush went to intensely fine detail and yet the finished work was always an artistic whole and never like a photograph. He was a naturalist from the time he could walk, and passing through the egg-collecting period he developed a deep reverence for life before he went up to Cambridge to study medicine. After serving as a member of Scott's *Discovery* expedition to the Antarctic, 1901-1904, Wilson was appointed field naturalist to the Commission on the Investigation of Grouse Disease. This was an early example of a scientific naturalist being engaged to help solve a definite problem and this he and his colleagues did well. Once more, Wilson's technique as a painter was valuable and his coloured representations of plumage of grouse in various stages of disease are as good as any coloured photographs of to-day. He left with Scott for the Antarctic again in 1910, and this was the end of his work in natural history in Britain. Henceforth he was immersed in original work on Antarctic birds and seals, in which he made the terrible journey with Bowers and Cherry-Garrard to get eggs of the Emperor penguin. Revering life as he did, Wilson would never hesitate to kill for food or knowledge, and anyone who has had to butcher seals in the interests of science will know how affecting an experience that can be to a sensitive mind. Edward Wilson was what other great naturalists have been, a great man.

We have lost several good naturalists in recent years, like J. G. Millais and Archibald Thorburn. Both men painted and drew animals showing great naturalness of posture and movement. Both produced monumental works, and both

W. H. HUDSON 1841-1922
Oil painting by Sir William Rothenstein

were well known shooting men. Edmund Selous was very much the opposite, being violently antagonistic to blood sports. This man emphasized the technique of closely observing one bird or a pair for a long period and of interpreting behaviour with severe logic. Unfortunately he had a style of English which is exasperating to read, so that such books as *The Evolution of Habit in Birds*, 1933, are heavy going.

Eliot Howard, who has died within the last year, set himself the task of probing the bird's mind, though I am sure his modesty would not let him think he would ever solve the problem. He was a man of means who used his leisure well in long and arduous birdwatching. He was the first to show the close relation between territory and reproduction and went on to demonstrate the role of avian display in synchronizing breeding condition between a pair of birds. I feel that the deeper Howard got into his subject the more awed he became at the beauty he was discovering. His last books *The Nature of a Bird's World*, 1935, and *A Waterhen's World*, 1940, show an almost mystical appreciation of nature, yet his methods were scientifically searching and his interpretation entirely disciplined. From the very nature of their subject and the complete lack of window dressing, Howard's books are not easy reading, but their prose has a majesty which will place them in the body of English literature.

The part played by local natural history societies should not be overlooked. These bodies collected assiduously in the half century when we hardly knew what we had. The members watched animals and published data which later workers have found useful. The societies are now in decline throughout the country and we may attribute the reason in part to the fact that there is less semi-skilled collecting to do, and partly to the high technique now necessary in the pursuit of natural history. All the same, if the amateur can spare the time he can contribute valuable observational studies of living things towards given ends and it may be supposed that it will be along such lines the natural history societies will gather new life.

Wood engraving from Bewick's *Fables*, c. 1779

NOCTULE : BROWN BAT
Lithograph by Lodge from Millais' *Mammals of Great Britain and Ireland*, 1904-1906

THE PRESENT AND THE FUTURE

THIS is no full review of British naturalists, but it will serve to show the emergence of natural history from the pragmatic lore of the hunter and amusement of the sportsman to the mental and physical discipline of men on their spiritual journey through life. Natural History is now a scientific study and the attitude of a growing number of people towards wild life is that of Albert Schweitzer's philosophy of respect and reverence for life. But an attitude in itself is not enough in a changing countryside to conserve and regulate its wild life. Positive action is needed also, based not only on the new sentiment but on the facts of science. The liberal-minded observer of scientific work takes the view that there is no *pure* research : there is the search for knowledge and some knowledge is of more immediate practical application ; the rest fits in in its own time. Justification of this point of view is evident many times over in a study of wild-life conservation. The naturalist has joined with the mathematician, the pathologist and the physiologist to produce a beautiful flowering of knowledge of the world about us. This knowledge of principles, of how things work, is constantly being

FOX

Engraving from the Rev. W. Bingley's *Memoirs of British Quadrupeds*, 1809

extended by research, but its full power will come only when it is applied to the lives of plants, animals and men, each in relation to the other.

The most obvious step towards wild-life conservation appears to be the establishment of sanctuaries—this is what William the Conqueror did. Many honest well-wishers of wild life have not progressed beyond this admittedly excellent 900-year-old technique. What they do not realise is that there are fifty times the number of people in Britain now. Reserves and sanctuaries alone are not effective in such a small and heavily populated country as Britain, without careful management. Management is scientific gamekeeping or the application of the science of ecology. This is the least arrogant of all sciences for its followers seek knowledge from men of lowly estate as humbly as from some great master, for be it known that the mind of an intelligent but illiterate man is a brilliant thing and lovely. It observes minutely and accurately, remembers and correlates, and its shining facets are untarnished by the mazing facts of the printed page. The ecologist of to-day is the academic hunter, liberated from the need to kill and able to extend and enfold in his search for knowledge, so that his science becomes that of being able to forecast consequences.

Ecology of plants was studied in Britain before the science was applied to animal life, and it is characteristic of ecology that those who follow each branch should be in closest co-operation. Those doyens of ecological botany, Professors Salisbury and Tansley, have been the needful friends of a struggling and in many ways more difficult animal ecology in Britain which has developed in the last twenty years.

OTTER
Lithograph from William Daniell's *Animated Nature*, 1809

It is a bold but justifiable simplification to say that animal ecology resolves itself into a study of the inter-relations of and fluctuations of numbers of animals. This was the approach of Charles Elton, now Director of the Bureau of Animal Population, University of Oxford. His initial academic research into the fluctuations of vole populations has led him and several others into an immense field of work, much of which has immediate application to problems of human life. In addition to the research done from Oxford, the Bureau has become a sensitive touch on the pulse of wild-life investigations throughout the world.

The successful future of British wild life, then, depends on the will of the people to set aside reserves or sanctuaries and to apply intelligently the gathering fund of scientific knowledge. But in that phrase "the will of the people" is meant a good deal more than an impersonal acquiescence in the state or some public body proclaiming an area to be a wild-life reserve. It means an attitude of mind as well, a vivid interestedness which sees and loves, and desires to care for that which is loved, whether it be in a reserve or in a garden. Indeed, laws made ahead of the will of the people are of little avail to the end to which they are designed. This attitude of mind is present in varying strata of society, but its expression varies much from district to district. Some of the areas richest in wild life and which would be the natural sites for sanctuaries receive no positive care or interest from the human inhabitants, though sometimes a cell of active opinion can create a pride, and a public sense of honour that a countryside should be the place chosen by certain species for their home or resting place. Take the example of North Norfolk, one of the finest bird grounds in England:

there are terns and waders at Scolt Head, Blakeney Point and other places on the coast, marsh-loving birds in the Broads, including the bittern, and a fine variety of duck on the fresh and salt water of the neighbourhood. The Norfolk Naturalists' Trust and the Royal Society for the Protection of Birds run most of the sanctuaries, and the propaganda of these bodies has been excellent, suffusive but never intrusive. The result is that the great majority of people in that area is proud of the birds and takes an intelligent interest in them. A friend of mine went to spend a week in the district expressly to do some birdwatching and on his way back to his inn one evening he was hailed by a working man digging in his garden—what luck among the birds? My friend remarked on having seen golden-eye duck for the first time in his life and was much satisfied.

"Did you see a Barrow's among them?" asked the man.

My friend had been pleased enough with the golden-eye alone, but this man had gone far beyond that stage and could, apparently, have detected the presence of the rare Barrow's golden-eye had it been there among the others. That same friend was passed from hand to hand and permitted to see an ibis which then had its temporary abode in the ditches of that flat region. The folk of the countryside knew the ibis was there but they were taking good care what strangers were to be allowed to see it. We may say that in that district with its moderately heavy rural human population and its many human activities, wild life is in good hands and will be able to persist or even increase. And in a way the bird life of North Norfolk is helping to repay its debt to the people by attracting an increasing number of tourists in the best sense of the word. This is a fact to which we must face up and not adopt an exclusive and precious attitude: wild life has money value for the country it inhabits and rightly exploited this tourist interest has great cultural possibilities.

The Highlands of Scotland can show the other side of the picture; though be it said there are many Highlanders who do take pride in the rich fauna of their wild country and care for it. But it is difficult to preserve a sanctuary in the area: many of the natives are ignorant of the names of the birds they see about them and are only too eager to pick up a pound for every grey-lag goose egg which can be produced for well-to-do visitors, and to point to the lochs where the black- and red-throated divers breed. Sea birds provide cheap shooting for a certain type of launch party and throughout the West Highlands there is a lack of any notion of conservation, or of wise use of natural resources. The deer forests do provide sanctuary for many creatures if their credentials show them not to interfere with sport.

Thus the wild cat remains common and I should say the pine marten is tending to increase rather than decrease. Several owners and tenants of Sutherland properties, where it is most common, have agreed not to trap or shoot the marten; and this has been done privately without any promptings from societies interested in preservation.

The creation of wild-life sanctuaries in Britain has been mainly the enterprise of individuals and relatively small and impecunious societies. There is no con-

By courtesy of Mrs. Thorburn

POLECAT
Coloured lithograph by A. Thorburn
From Millais' *Mammals of Great Britain and Ireland*, 1904-1906

By courtesy of Mrs. Millais

GREY SEAL

Coloured lithograph by J. G. Millais

siderable area of ground in Britain which has been set aside by the state as a wild-life reserve first and foremost. The state has definitely lagged behind, though probably no country has talked so much about wild-life protection, appointed committees to investigate the subject of national parks and so on, and done less. The latest example of this technique of talk, but without a pound of good money to do, is the establishment of a House of Lords Committee to co-ordinate the many diffuse elements interested in conserving wild life. We shall not get national parks without the expenditure of a goodly sum of hard cash and so far there is little evidence that the British Government has any intention of placing national parks among the earlier items of post-war reconstruction. It does not seem to be realized that a series of national parks in Britain would have an immense social value for the community, quite apart from the value as wild-life sanctuaries. At the moment, I think public opinion is ahead of the Government in this matter and though regretting the lack of impetus which state action could give, it may be taken as a healthy sign that the public is growing eager ; when national parks do come they will be treated with more care and a sense of gratitude by the people.

Let us see what protection is being given at present and the mode of administration. All royal parks are bird sanctuaries, a fact of no small importance when we think of the parkland and scrub these areas contain, and the expanses of reedy water such as Duddingston Loch in the King's Park, Edinburgh. The properties administered by the National Trust are mainly rural ones and though not sanctuaries *ipso facto* they are treated as such as far as possible. One of their island properties, the Calf of Man, is specially a bird sanctuary where a warden lives to exercise authority if necessary, but there is some danger of this limited area of cliff and island being over-visited by an enthusiastic public. Many municipal authorities protect the creatures within their parks, but passively. The Royal Society for the Protection of Birds is active in caring for certain areas occupied by particular rare birds—for example, the sanctuary for the Kentish plover at Dungeness and the headland of Hermaness in Shetland where the Society's timely action undoubtedly saved the great skua from extinction as a British breeding bird.

Local societies like the one in Norfolk already mentioned exercise some protection, but shortage of funds is usually a limiting factor to the fine efforts of the individuals who give freely of their time and energy in the work. Particular groups or even pairs of birds such as the British kites are cared for by the Association of Bird Watchers and Wardens. Societies such as those for the Promotion of Nature Reserves, and the Preservation of the Fauna of the Empire, do not administer sanctuaries themselves but they help to co-ordinate efforts of individuals and governments and undertake propaganda.

Many individuals, rich and not very rich, make sanctuaries of their policies or gardens and the influence of these small islands of relative safety must be considerable. A good old garden provides so much nesting cover and feeding surface for birds and owners usually augment these advantages by providing food and water, as well as nesting boxes for those species which will use them. Birds are obvious and beautiful things and their friends are legion, but we need an extension of this private habit of protection to other classes of animals. Supposing the owners of riparian rights of a whole river and any fishing associations or syndicates concerned were to say to themselves—here is a very special thing, a river, water running now fast, now slow, through a variety of country, but preserving a continuity: these related habitats of steep banks, rapids and pools; alder canopies and water meadows; of reeds and flags, and of broad estuary, attract and hold a fauna and flora of great richness beyond that of the country between rivers. If these individuals and groups were to say that, and thereupon frame a policy of live and let live, their influence for good would be enormous. The insect life of river systems is for the most part not harmful to human activities; it is affected to some extent by the plant life of rivers, not necessarily in providing food plants above water but as a maker and maintainer of underwater habitats as well. This vast invertebrate life feeds the fish of the rivers and some of the birds like the dipper, the swallow, the common sandpiper, the warblers and the wagtails. And the fish at varying stages of their growth feed other fish such as pike and cannibal trout, some birds, like kingfisher, heron, merganser and cormorant. The otter is also feeding on fish and sometimes on the birds that use the river. Rivers are pathways of animal life, even as they were the first roads of human beings. The banks and muddy places show the passage of weasel and stoat, of water vole and water shrew and of wading birds. What a vast complex of life is in the hands of river owners and users! Little or any of it need be destroyed because there is food and sport for all concerned; only cormorant and merganser need be discouraged, perhaps, because they can live well enough on the fish of the salt water.

Again, if every owner of a wood were to look upon it as a reservoir of wild life, and in those right and proper measures of good forestry try to leave one bit always that had not too great a density of trees, but had some underwood as well and even a few dead branches rotting on the ground. The farmer and gardener are deepest in debt to the birds and these men should look upon their thorn hedges and hedgerow timber as the cover needed by the birds for nesting and for retreat. The thrusting man who grubs all his hedges to make big fields is not necessarily adding to the efficiency of farming. There is no shelter for beast or bird in a temporary wire fence. I have spudded thistles in a field of young corn with a hard-bitten old farmer who carefully left one of these noxious weeds growing because it was sheltering a lark's nest, and in any late harrowings of the arable ground he would quarter the fields first to find the peewits' nests and mark them with sticks so that the steel spikes should not break and scatter them.

Owners of sandpits, brickworks, quarries and the like can with a little imagination and no inconvenience let their delvings be to the advantage of the wild life of the district. How soon do the sandmartins, the wagtails, the hawks and many another creature find the artificial banks, heights and pools of such places.

These are activities in which every one of us can help by a little forethought and care, and it is worth remembering that the fate of wild life in a land of surging humanity devolves on all of us as individuals; the state can help in many ways, but the state is only the collective authoritative voice of individual men and women.

VOLE
Etching by Winifred Austen

Let us try for a few moments to visualize what a British wild-life policy might do. National parks are a prime need : one for the whole of Britain would not be enough, for it is obvious no single tract of ground manageable as a park would cover the varied types of habitat which we have seen this country provides. There could be many small parks comprising such places as parts of Exmoor, the Cornish and Devon coasts, parts of the New Forest, a piece of the Downs, a representative area of fen and broad, good English woodland as is to be found in the Midlands, the Welsh islands and a Yorkshire moor. Lest I be misunderstood let me say at once that I do not expect any government to spend immense sums of money acquiring such places, evicting the human inhabitants to create small wildernesses which will lose a lot of money. These small parks would be designed to serve as museum pieces in a countryside which will certainly change in the years to come. Agriculture, forestry and all other human works would continue and the areas should pay their way, or almost do so as landed estates are run at present. Some emphasis would be laid on giving wild life its chance, excluding rabbits and rats which would so soon interfere with normal rural life. No special attempt would be made to encourage large numbers of people into these restricted areas, or the very purpose they serve would be nullified. It would be realized that in these areas man is part of the ecological complex, his passive influence neither to be deplored nor exaggerated, but accepted.

There are other districts which call for schedule as national parks not because of their intrinsic value as wild-life reserves but as national lungs. Snowdonia, the English Lakes and the Cairngorm region are examples, and there are certain smaller pieces of country like the Peak district which need protection against exploitation. The main purpose of such potential national parks is outwith the scope of this essay, though their incidental value as sanctuaries should not be lost to sight.

There remains to be established a definite wild-life reserve of large size in cheap and almost empty country, and the only place remaining in Britain where this could be done is the West and Northern Highlands. The very remoteness and difficult nature of the terrain would add to its value as a reserve. Wild coast, island, sea loch, lake and estuary ; mountain glen and river ; pine wood, birch and primitive oak scrub ; all are there in plenty except woodland which could be easily increased by fencing small areas and allowing natural regeneration of the trees which are presently kept low by the grazing of deer and sheep. By management, this wild-life reserve would be expected to hold most of our land mammals, many beautiful insect species, more kinds of birds than there are at present, and more of our native flora.

Now this reserve will be the property of the British people and they will wish to enjoy it in the best sense of the word. The number of people entering the reserve annually may be expected to run to tens of thousands, so if the area is to fulfil its aim as a sanctuary it will have to be very large by British standards—though still extremely small by American and Canadian standards—say a quarter of a million acres. The rights of the crofters on the seaward fringe would have to be safeguarded, and as far as possible the few farmers would continue their normal activities ; the deer forest ground would provide the inviolable sanctuary. Zoning of the area would give room for general recreation, a certain amount of licensed sport, and the untouched, undisturbed sanctuaries in which research on wild life could be conducted. In addition to this mainland area, outlying islands of particular faunal and floral value would be incorporated into the reserve—North Rona and Sula Sgeir for example, with their great stocks of Atlantic grey seals, their Leach's fork-tailed petrels and magnificent gannetry and cliffs of sea birds ; there is probably no other half square mile of British land so rich in wild life. There are nearer, more accessible islands, such as the Treshnish group, Colonsay and Ailsa Craig which would provide for the visitor some of the wonders of remote Sula Sgeir and North Rona. The fantastically beautiful island group of St. Kilda is already a private sanctuary for birds which include the distinctive St. Kilda wren, and for its mammals—the sub-specific house mouse and long-tailed fieldmouse, and the primitive Soay sheep which is nearest the moufflon in type of any British sheep.

A national reserve of the character outlined would be a busy place, catering for its visitors, caring for the agriculture and social life of the area in which it is

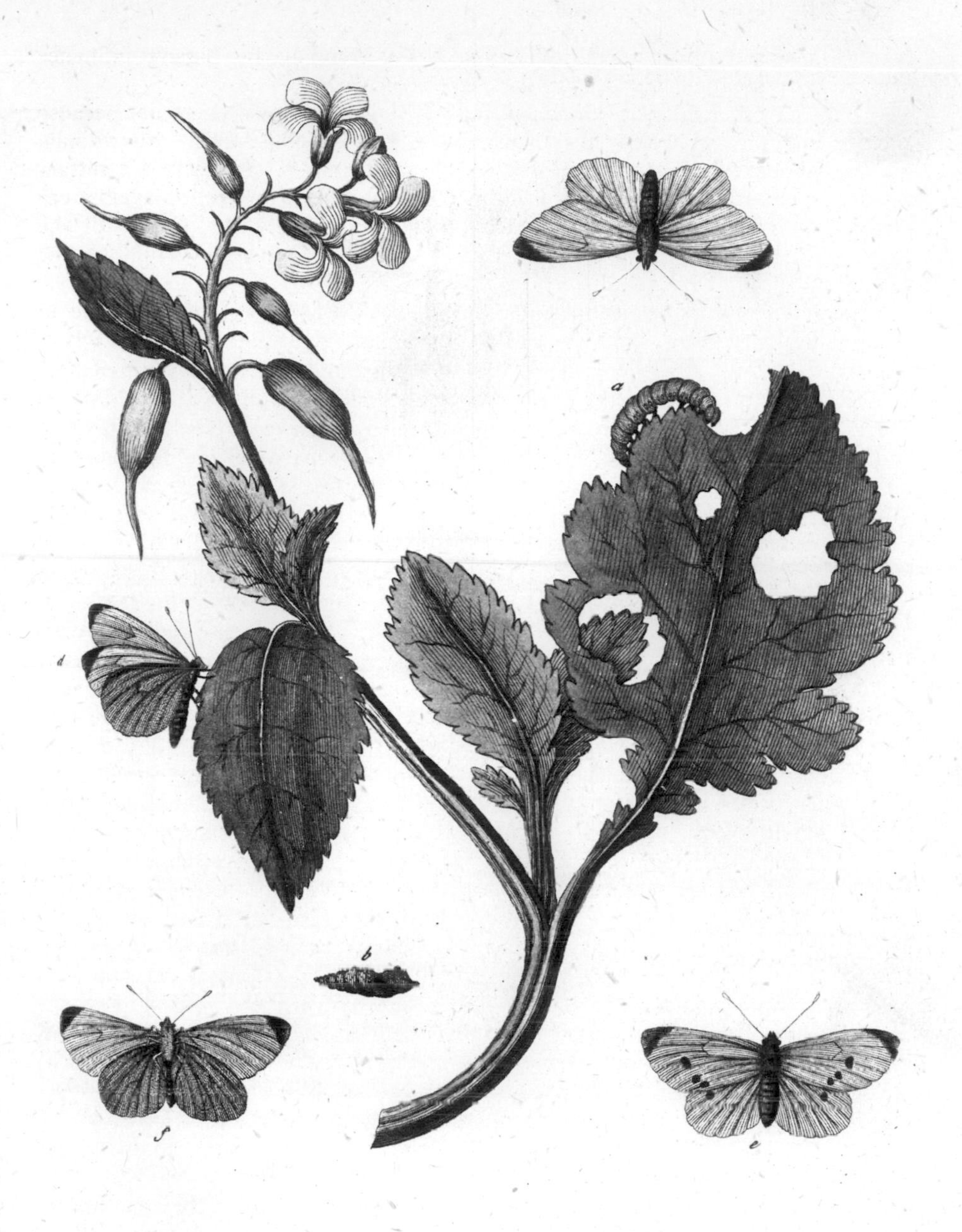

CABBAGE WHITE BUTTERFLIES
Engraving from Terasson after Albin
From Eleazar Albin's *Natural History of English Insects*, 1720

placed, running a big research programme and giving forth of its knowledge and outlook culturally, to become integral in the nation's life.

Here then, is Britain, with its human inhabitant for every acre of ground, yet possessing a heritage of wild life which no European country can equal, and for its size and limitations few countries in the world. This heritage will remain only if we make positive effort to conserve it, each in his own way. At the apex of this effort would be a group of research workers in animal ecology, animal sociology and behaviour, and plant ecology. Perhaps they will be banded together ultimately in a body akin to the United States Bureau of Biological Survey, yet acting as independent men of science and buffered in some way from direct civil service control. The core of such a body exists now in the Bureau of Animal Population already mentioned as having worked particularly on the field vole (*Microtus agrestis*). That vole research, which in itself has produced results of practical value in forestry, agriculture and medicine, has led to new methods of rodent control. At the outbreak of the present war, much of the Bureau's energy was turned to destruction of rabbits and rats and the methods evolved are proving far more effective and decisive than those of the gamekeeper and ratcatcher. Since the war research into control of the woodpigeon has been inaugurated at the Edward Grey Institute of Ornithology, University of Oxford. This is practically the first time economic ornithology has received official recognition in Britain. Long before the war Dr. W. Collinge had conducted a laborious research on the food of birds, a work which was of direct practical value, but which still needs amplification. Sound knowledge on all these points would prevent such foolish and harmful measures as that of agricultural bodies giving a bounty for sparrows' eggs collected by children.

In addition to the Bureau of Animal Population, other bodies are also conducting ecological research on wild stocks of animals. Captain Cyril Diver, a clerk to the House of Commons, has for many years studied the ecology of Studland Heath, Dorset, with the help of amateurs. There is also the Freshwater Biological Station, at Wray Castle, Windermere, under the well known ecologist E. B. Worthington. The Marine Biological Stations and Research Laboratories at Plymouth, Lowestoft, Millport (Ayrshire) and Aberdeen, study the life of the sea, but their work extends far beyond British territorial waters.

This science of ecology can help to build up stocks of mammals, and as I see it, some representatives of the British fauna could help to pay for the research and care which would be expended on wild life as a whole. There is nothing shameful in wise use of the material value of certain animals, indeed it is to be encouraged when such use results in increased stocks.

The red deer is an example where toll is already taken to the advantage of the species as a whole. Similar toll could be taken of Atlantic seals, basking sharks, gannets, fulmar petrels and the eggs of gulls. In the course of writing this essay I have received a letter from a firm which uses a thousand pounds weight of eider down each year: eider down is now difficult to get and I was asked if there is any hope of augmenting the short supply from British sources.

RED DEER
Wood engraving from Bewick's *History of Quadrupeds*, 1807

Now the eider duck is increasing in numbers here and extending its range southwards; we could take advantage of this natural surge of a species by giving it the active protection which the Icelanders and Norwegians give to encourage the eider duck to nest in little shelters of stones. This practice not only localizes the nests but is a definite check on the egg-stealing of the great black-backed gulls. There are hundreds of islets on our West Highland coasts where the wild eider duck could be "farmed" and its first plucking of down gathered for commerce. No life would be taken; instead, those who would gather the down would pay attention to ensuring the safe passage of the eider ducklings from the nest to the sea, a journey at present fraught with danger; and with a duck which is naturally so tame and kindly, I see no reason why those who live by the shore in suitable places should not successfully rear and breed eider ducks, allowing them full freedom to feed in the sea.

The Oxford ecologists have given much time to studying the dynamics of population of a few wild and laboratory stocks of animals. The methods of obtaining these vital statistics are adaptations of human actuarial technique and are applicable to other wild animals. James Fisher, the writer of *The Birds of Britain* in this series, has studied the fulmar petrel in this way, and with friends is collecting the material for a statistical study of the gannet. The writer of this essay has collected data on red deer, Atlantic seals and on some species of gulls. At present, all this information is academic, but it would be of practical value immediately the nation looked upon wild life as sharing our own destiny. That is the point, we are all animals together and we, being human and capable of reflection, ought to sort out our relations one to another with the scientific techniques becoming available. Let us have no over-sentimentalizing of wild animals, refusing to take life and trying always to remove the influence of man ; this attitude is almost as wrong as considering any living thing as fair game and exploiting the stock until it is gone. I tried earlier in this essay to define the attitude of the hunter before the dawn of agriculture, as one loving his beasts and his country though he continually hunted to kill. He did share his world with the animals and realized their value to him ; and we, in an age of plastics and synthetic fibres, can still find room for some of the ancient hunter's common sense, and add to our regard an ennobling awareness born of growing knowledge

HERON
Etching by J. Wycliffe Taylor
From St. John's *Natural History and Sport in Moray*, 1882